The Time Between The Tides

~

A Journal

~~~~~~~~~~~~~~~~~~~

Maggie Lea

IBSN 978-0-9828754-0-7

Copyright © 2010 Maggie Lea

All rights reserved. No part of this book may be reproduced by any means or in any form whatsoever without written permission from the publisher, except for brief quotations embodied in literary articles or reviews. For additional information, write to:

Lea Press
5810 Kahiliholo Road
Kilauea, HI 96754-5112

For Saim,
who sets me on the seas,
time after time.

Preface

I was swimming out into the middle of a wide channel in Turkey when on that early morning watching the sunrise I felt that deep water stillness when you are aware it is the time between the tides. It is that safe place of waiting in-between the comings and goings. That place where the old and new haven't shown up yet in all their fullness. That pregnant moment when you still feel anything is possible. It is neither full nor empty it is just that blissful place of enough. Yes, that moment of peace where there is just enough. How sweet when the sun rises on such a day and you rest your heart and soul in its silent spaciousness. On such a day you feel a slowing down that takes you into a deeper acceptance of the I don't knows of your life. You bear witness as this inner compass finally settles down and centers you into your own true **N**orth, even while facing **E**ast. A moment when all you truly know is you are home. Home at long last from your journey on the seas of the ebb and flow of life. This is a book and your journal about being in that stillness of the in-between, the pause before you venture out once again, or maybe are found out, seen for who you are. And anyone who has been seen in such a way knows how that makes all the difference and sets you on the seas once again. But that's another book, another journal all to itself. For now it is enough to just be in the stillness of the in-between.

Maggie Lea

N
W + E
S

Full Moon
Kalihiwai Ridge
Kaua`i, Hawai`i

Journal Entries

The Time Between The Tides 1

True North 9

Home 15

Rest 21

Slowing Down 27

Stop 33

I Don't Know 39

Waiting 47

Between the Comings and Goings 53

Between the Old and New 59

Neither Full Nor Empty 65

Just Enough 71

Silence 77

Spaciousness 85

Safe Place 91

Anything Is Possible 97

Pregnant Moments 103

Peace 109

Stillness of the In-between 115

time – past, present or future; every moment there has ever been or ever will be; finite duration; measurable interval

between – in or through the space or time that separates two things; along a course that connects or relates to; in the interval

tides – the alternate rise and fall of the surface of oceans, seas, bays, rivers; caused by the attraction of the moon and sun; the period during which something is at its highest or lowest point

The Time Between The Tides

Life is an ebb and flow. We live in cycles and phases and there are times between these tides that create their own movement, their own pause. It is here where the movement of life is so subtle we can hardly detect its effect.

It is the quality, and yes quantity of these times we write about here. For this is my journal and yours to go into these subtle places, no matter how deep or shallow, both are important. To go deep or to have breadth in life, there is a place for both. To stay on the surface of things or get to the bottom, sometimes to hit bottom, when life throws you an unexpected curve, a blow, or perhaps you have just had it. It is here we come.

It is time to recognize and honor at whatever level you find yourself, that your life may have reached a moment where you no longer wish to ignore this subtle turning. No matter whether this turning is away from or towards, going out to sea or coming back home, saying yes, or finally saying no. Listening to and feeling the messages of this time between the tides is what calls you and me to our own connection to what is, whatever that might be, to wherever it might lead us.

As a young child I used to believe the tides were caused by ships that went far out to sea, and at certain times they would put Tide™ laundry detergent into the sea. During high tides when the surf was rough and foamy that meant there had been detergent released from these ships.

I don't exactly know when it became clear to me that it was the attraction of our sun and moon and not the Tide ships that caused our tides to be high or low, but it was my first realization there were forces in nature and events in life beyond our control. We are at the mercy of forces greater than us more often in our lives than we might care to admit, and to navigate through these high and low tides often requires great skill and sometimes even greater courage. Only later did I come to understand what was more important than anything else was the love required to stay the course of one's own life. Love for all of our selves, and for all the others in our life, who come and go in and out of our journey, as we navigate the highs and lows of living and of being fully alive.

As the years have passed, and I have been blessed with many, the time between the tides has become more and more important to me. I'm living in the numbered years now where I'm more aware there is much less of it for me than what I have already lived. I think this realization has created a greater value for the more subtle moments than I felt in my youth. Times then I would not have even noticed.

Now is all important. Not missing any of it. That is why feeling the stillness of the time between the tides out in that channel in Turkey was so important to me. I had arrived at a new level of awareness and sensitivity.

It was like an upgraded radar system had been installed in me so I could finally receive these more subtle messages I had been ignoring for so long and could ignore no longer.

I don't believe in the Tide ships anymore, but I have come to love our sun and moon that direct the tides and am glad they are so much a part of our lives. These pages reflect especially the dark moon phase of when we feel that time between the tides and know a new moon, a new life is forming. We can be a part of that new phase if we connect our consciousness to this time, these moments of the in-between. For it is here we actually become the co-creators of our life and can stay the course or steer our ship to go elsewhere. Going out to sea once again before we are called back home one last time.

~ Journal for The Time Between The Tides ~

true – faithful; loyal; constant; reliable; certain; agrees with reality; accurate; right; correct; genuine; authentic; honest

north – the direction to the right of a person facing the sunset; the needle of a compass points to the magnetic north pole rather than to the geographic pole; the point on a compass at zero degree or 360 degrees directly opposite south

True North

I was at a gathering where we were confused about the direction we were facing, as living on a nearly circular island you don't always have a clear sense of this, and so I am never without my compass. Much to my surprise, when we sought its counsel, we knew it was wrong. Finding true north was no longer possible as apparently my compass had lost its magnetism, its connection to the earth's magnetic poles. I never knew that it was possible for a compass not to be able to find its way. For a compass to be lost or give out wrong information unnerved, and yes, saddened me. I was naive in thinking a compass would always work, would always be true for me. Unless it was smashed I always believed in my compass. Now I had to question even this.

We all know times in our life where it feels like we have lost our way, have lost touch with our own true north and have taken a wrong turn. It seems our inner guidance system is broken somehow or is no longer connected to whatever our source is that moves us clearly forward on our chosen path. We may not be on our path anymore, may even feel totally lost in someone else's world, and wonder how to find our way home. We might be at a standstill or at a crossroads in our life where knowing true north becomes essential. It is here when we know the time has come to press on again and either change course or get back on course as we continue our journey home.

Because there is a sense of going home in this life, or in feeling at home, that seems to require an inner sense of knowing your true north. Knowing you can settle into the center of your being and find a certain stillness and clarity that is in alignment with your truth, your values, your dreams coming true. When disconnected from this connection to center, to the ground of your being, finding true north is impossible. This leaves you disoriented and at the mercy of the other, the winds of fate, set cycles, or being controlled in ways that feel like your life is no longer your own.

Free will is always available, but the choices you make are now subject to more of what is going on outside rather than being able to take a true inner reading of what's happening in your selves. This awareness allows you to move from a place of I am that I am and now need and or want to be in the here and now of this. Being connected to your own true north allows you to navigate through your life in your own time and way, keeping you on course as you find and live out your ever shifting and changing life purpose.

Because of free will in ourselves and others change is a given. By keeping your inner compass magnetized and connected to your personal polar opposites it allows your own true north to be of more accurate service to you in either finding or keeping you on your own chosen path. This then gives you the assurance you are living the life you were called to live in all its fullness. Staying the course can then be navigated as your own unique adventure of discovery rather than going on chance wanderings in and out of exile and return.

~ Journal for True North ~

home – where one lives; dwelling place; the place where one was born or reared; place where one likes to be; restful or congenial; comfortable; at ease; familiar; a natural environment; to the center or the heart of a matter

Home

"I am home", aren't those amazing words. When you can say that and truly mean it something actually happens inside that allows you to let go and be more open, more in touch with yourself. When I consciously walk through my front door and close it behind me, it's like I have entered a refuge from the world, entering a world of my own making instead. I have come home.

This also happens for me in other ways, in some parts of nature, being with my mate, a close friend or my pets, driving in my car, going to my gazebo where I work, taking my boat out on the lake, or sometimes when traveling. All are situations where I feel at home, because home for me is about being open. It is being in a place or with a person or an animal where I feel open. Not necessarily relaxed always, or any specific feeling, but rather open to all possible feelings. A place where I feel safe to be openly myself and accepted not judged or controlled.

Home is more than where your heart is. It's where all of you can feel alive and, for now, you own it. It 'belongs' to you. A claim has been made, a commitment given, that for a time this feels like home. This is where my things are and what goes on here is meaningful or familiar and I respond with a kind of letting go to that place where I trust.

Playing house as a child I remember trying to have all my dolls and stuffed animals feel at home. My room was a refuge from family and the world, a private place where I first learned to be at home with myself. I closed that door and my room came alive for me. I would rearrange it and my imagination was born there where I would read or play or daydream for hours by myself. I was home. Then, most evenings in my early childhood, my Dad would bring me a warm glass of milk, tuck me into bed, say sweet dreams, and to this day that is probably as home as it gets, just the memory of that helps me feel safely at home.

Only recently have I come to be more at home in my body. I was always tall for my age and never quite fit in or fit the mold, but now this home for my soul is very precious to me. As I age, I love her more than ever as I am aware we will have to part company someday. Until then she's the only game in town. Without my body I wouldn't be here. That seems so obvious, so simple, but when you're not at home in your body there is a disconnection from being able to feel truly at home anywhere. It is in our body that we feel this life we're living, and being at ease with all those feelings is a big part of knowing when you're home. So as I connect more to feeling at home in my body I feel I've now finally come home to myself in the larger world as well, not just to that early childhood room where for me it all began.

~ Journal for Home ~

rest – peace, ease, and refreshment as produced by sleep; repose, refreshing ease or inactivity after work or exertion; a period or occasion of inactivity, as during work or on a journey; relief from anything distressing, annoying, tiring; peace of mind; mental and emotional calm; tranquility; state of being still; immobility; a resting or stopping place; to remain without change or further action

Rest

It is not often we find true rest. Even our sleep can be restless rather than full. To have enough time where you are at rest or are rested is not truly valued in our culture. That part of us that says "it's time to stop or at least slow down" is often put down or muted. You are not considered ambitious enough or your hard working self just won't allow it.

However, for our bodies, if we are listening to and value them for the temples they are supposed to be, rest is of great importance. One third of our life is spent in what we hope each night is restful sleep. In that sleep our dreams come to us. If we are lucky we remember them and find amazing guidance for our life, all because we give this time of rest special priority.

The body requires rest to restore for the next day. Anyone who has experienced sleep deprivation knows not just how physically exhausting it is, but also how crazy making. The lack of mental clarity alone reveals why this and isolation are used in torture. It becomes torture to not get proper rest over time. Yet coming to rest, coming to a place of rest where you let go and do nothing and decide to value this, doesn't come naturally to most people.

If we see our bodies as a temple, then imagine your eyes as the two doors. When they are closed it's a signal to go inside, to enter in and rest in the temple. This time of taking sanctuary in your own body and honoring its need to restore and create new life, new cells, means we are to stop, to let go of all demands, surrender in trust that your body will breathe for you, beat your heart, circulate your blood, keep all in good order until you return to consciousness and wake up once again. For a time each day your body needs you to enter this unconscious world and rest in the knowledge that you are being taken care of. Your body is ministering to you as you sleep in readiness for the new day, the new dawn.

There is a deep gratitude that comes over me when I first lay down to sleep. It is a sinking into my self like no other time of the day. A letting go in knowing I have done all I could possibly do that day and I now welcome the dark and the night sounds that bring me to rest, to that precious restful sleep. This pause is the very act of entering an in-between every day of my life. It is literally going into the stillness of the in-between of my days, one to the other, so I can know each will be unique and different and new, and yes, possibly full of unexpected surprises. Coming to rest and being rested are built into the very rhythm of life so we can benefit from our body's desire to take care of us. "As I lay me down to sleep. . ."

~ Journal for Rest ~

slowing – taking a longer time than is expected or usual to act, move, go or happen; not hasty, quick, ready or prompt; making relatively little progress for the time spent; holding back fast progress, development; characterized be little activity or lacking in energy

down – from a higher to a lower place; toward the ground; to a less excited or active condition; into a tranquil or quiet state

Slowing Down

Slowing down as opposed to speeding up. How strange we know exactly how to do that when driving a car but how foreign it can be when applying this action to our life. And it is an act. It is a decision to slow down. Not to halt what we're doing necessarily, but to slow down the pace of our lives. To realize there is a pace different than full speed ahead and that this other pace individual to us, has value. It is something we have to find in ourselves. It doesn't always come naturally to us in our culture and in today's world, where pressing on is essential if you want to keep up, and not be trampled on by the hordes you feel at your back.

There is a mob-like consciousness that can take over our life and shove all 'lesser' priorities out of the way.

In this consciousness the sensitivities needed to signal "it's time to slow down" get trampled. For some people they have been trampled beyond recognition, sometimes to their death.

Some of us seem to have no inner guidance that honors slowing down, let alone coming in for a landing. Perhaps because slowing down requires us to be grounded, to not just be in touch with our bodies, but to be in our bodies, embodied. Now those are words that fast and speedy have run right over. The very nature of embodiment means we are in touch with our inner guidance and our feelings. We listen to this guidance and honor our feelings when they say "slow down". We know from experience if we don't pay attention now there will be consequences to pay later. The very act of slowing down can actually bring us to the place we need to be faster than speeding up does to get us there.

Why is this? Because slowing down makes sure we don't pass up the necessary steps and places in our lives that can't be skipped without paying a high price later. Often a toll on our bodies is the first sign we have been going too fast. It is often our bodies that first tell us to slow down. A symptom shows up that we can't ignore any longer and slowing down can remedy this symptom, if we're lucky. If we listen to our feelings and embody ourselves at long last, there will be much reward and more gained as we notice what pace is healthier for us, and in acting on that knowledge, our life has more value because we are more fully living it, fully embodied.

~ Journal for Slowing Down ~

stop – to block up a passage, road, pipe; obstruct; to close; to prevent movement or further movement; to cease or intercept transit; to tarry or stay for a while; check; arrest; cessation; halt; coming to an end

Stop

Stop. I love words and playing with them. The word "stop" is "pots" spelled backwards. That means absolutely nothing profound as compared to "desserts" being "stressed" spelled backwards, which gives you something to chew on. See what I mean. Or to realize that "stop" can be one of those stand alone words that make a complete sentence.

Finding a word within words is another game I play, as in "to", "top", "sop", "pot", "sot". Where am I going with all this, you might ask? To be honest, I'm not quite sure. What I do know is that nearly every day of our lives we are exposed to the word "stop", and every day when we heed that word, in driving especially, we save ourselves from an accident waiting to happen at a crossroads that could be potentially very harmful to ourselves and/or to others. Learning how to stop is not only something we need at a very young age for our own safety, it is essential we learn it in greater depth as an adult.

There are times in life where our only option, our only choice, is to stop. Sometimes there is no other safe or wise thing for us to do. Stop what we're doing, being, thinking, feeling, needing, wanting, giving, taking, loving, hating, judging, controlling, hurting, worrying, playing, working, pushing, pulling, eating, drinking, and so on. To just stop, so as to be able to move on into the healthier, happier, safer, better way of life offered to us if we invest in this time of essential change.

Such change in life can come to us as a choice, or sometimes stopping feels imposed on us by circumstances beyond our control. Stopping requires us to know in some way how to stop. This knowledge comes as a moment of awareness where you realize it is time to cease all forward movement, put on the internal brakes, and know and believe it's now a good and beneficial time to stop.

That simple action can have a profound effect on the self and others. In that moment of stopping, a decision is made to halt a habit or pattern that creates aspects in our life that no longer work nor produce results we need for now, or might want for our future.

In order for the new to enter in, we are sometimes required to stop the old and enter a more centered place of awareness. This is where to stop, and nothing more, connects us to our own personal power of being able to consciously enter into a pause, perhaps even enter a potential sacred point of transformation. To take a break in life before life breaks us. To realize and feel the power and value of stopping, helps us to see that there are times in life where there is nothing that is more important, or could possibly top, stopping. It is enough to just stop, because to keep trying to top stop just keeps us going.

Stop.

~ Journal for Stop ~

don't – do not; in no manner, to no degree, often implying refusal to perform, to carry out, fulfill, to bring to completion, finish, cause or produce

know – to have a clear perception or understanding of; be sure of or well informed about; to be aware or cognizant of; have perceived or learned; to have a firm mental grasp of securely in the memory; to be acquainted or familiar with; to have understanding of or skill in as a result of study or experience; to recognize as distinct; distinguish; to be sure, informed or aware; to have intercourse with

I Don't Know

To come to the place of "I don't know" is to be set down in uncertainty where you are consciously aware of having no answers. The flow has stopped inside and out, and you really have no idea of what now or what next. You only know you've come to the end of something that fills you with such emptiness it takes your breath away. Because this leaves you so raw inside, staying with this kind of "I don't know" is often very difficult.

We are wired to want answers and to have things change in an evolving sort of way, but "I don't know" isn't about going forward. It is about being in the standstill. There is little movement here and yet life carries on with its mundane round of activity in spite of whether you know the next step or not. How long can you live with the ambiguity and confusion that "I don't know" brings? It often involves another person or decisions that have to be made and our tendency is to rush past uncertainty and to just try and fix it or come up with any kind of answers so as to feel in the flow again, to just do something.

But that solution can be short lived, and take you down paths you will just have to double back on later. The "I don't know" phases of our lives have actually stopped us on the path, and for a time we feel lost, sometimes abandoned by another or to the whims of fate.

It is here, stopped on the path, maybe at a crossroads, where a seed can be planted for new life, new growth, new direction. The old is dying off and you know at a deep place in your soul there is no turning back. There have been questions asked where the answer, for now, is honestly "I don't know." There are feelings taking you to new depths where nothing is familiar.

All you can do for sure is start to breathe again. Yes, breathe in and out, in the void of this "I don't know." This place where nothing is yet manifested, nothing is truly known. It is that empty place full of possibility where all you can do is trust that yes, even this moment will change and end. Time will then carry you on to a moment, when having stayed in the standstill long enough, the brain fog lifts and something finally becomes clear, becomes known.

It is here in this time and space where the prayer of "let it be easy" is finally answered and you are activated into a belief that this seed planted in the dark soil of your soul needs your tender loving care. This seed needs a time of standstill as you guard your mind and heart from any doubt that indeed it will germinate into the new form your life now must take.

It is this time of "I don't know" that is the preparation for this process of germination that ultimately reveals the knowing of what now and what next. The crossroads have been faced and a choice made. A conscious step out of the standstill is taken into a place in which you can say, "I know here there is real potential for new life, new growth, new direction." "I know what I know" replaces "I don't know" and you finally move on, feeling the flow of life moving you forward into the slow, but sure, revealing.

~ Journal for I Don't Know ~

waiting – to stay in a place or remain in readiness or anticipation until something expected happens; to be ready; to stop or wait for someone to catch up

Waiting

Ah waiting. How many times have you been told to wait, be patient? Told that all things change and end, so if you just wait it out, a whole new set of circumstances will present themselves for you to respond to. That you might just as well wait, because if you don't, you might just screw it all up even more than what you're waiting to pass, waiting to come, waiting to change, or just figuring out what it is you're waiting for period.

All this waiting we do in the name of "it can't get any worse" or "God, how could it possibly get any better than this?" Either place becomes a standstill of eventual waiting for when the worse gets better or the better gets worse. Or if you're an eternal optimist like me, waiting for the ever changing for the better. This is the time between the changes in our lives when we know if we wait, do or say nothing, make no intentions, and just let it be, maybe our waiting will have a certain kind of power.

This waiting for the universe to move on our behalf doesn't really need our help at this moment. It just needs us to stop and wait for the moment when we are called back into the flow of our life. Until then, waiting can take on a certain dignity. It has some manners to it, this kind of waiting. It's not our turn yet, and a part of us knows this by putting that restraining hand on our urges to do or say something, to make premature decisions, when it's really much wiser to just wait our turn. To listen for our name to be called back into whatever really belongs to us. Otherwise, whose life are we living? It is at least worth waiting for that true answer, don't you think? Or put another way, how does waiting help us find the life that belongs to us?

By allowing our life phases to ripen, we can sometimes enter into a process of more sensitive awareness that shows us a clearer definition of being in the beginning, middle or end of something. Then the pauses we live between an end and a new beginning can allow us to feel that ripeness in ways that nourish and inform our next choices. We pick the fruit from our own tree of knowledge more and more when that fruit is ripe for having waited. Living with respect for this waiting process, this ripening to occur is full of its own reward. A time of "letting it be" can then become a time of letting it ripen until what belongs to us is truly known and therefore more likely ours.

~ Journal for Waiting ~

coming – to move from a place thought of as there to a place thought of as here; approaching; immediately next; to become actual

going – to move along, travel, proceed; a leaving, a departure

Between the Comings and Goings

What does it really mean to come and go? We get so busy with the movement of our lives that the time between hardly has value. The arrival and departure often require so much planning and anticipation the life lived in-between can get lost in the constant thinking about where I've been and where I'm going.

This, of course, brings you to that moment of living what is now. It sounds so easy in all those books about being present in the moment, but it comes and goes so quickly. It seems as if all of life is a coming and going, so to be in-between all that isn't always clear.

Is it a place where we just hang out for awhile and suspend our selves in that lovely sense of nothingness? That blissful interlude when nothing is pushing or pulling us to be here or there, this or that, us or them. It is that blank space on the calendar where there is nothing to do, nowhere to go, and no one to see. No expectations at last. All this coming and going seems to stop us for a moment before the plans and the anticipations kick back in, and all there is between the two, is nothing. No thing to distract us from "the power of now".

It is so rich this moment of being fully in what is. Hard to describe or write about as it doesn't want to be penned down. Pardon the pun but actually that is a lot of what being in-between the comings and goings is all about. Not being pinned down like a butterfly on a specimen board. Our lives are not meant to be pinned down, becoming a specimen of "ourselves".

It is our awareness of this being in-between the activity of coming and going that is so special about being human. This self awareness that we can plan and anticipate and then let all that go and live what actually shows up, because it's not always what we expect. It is often **nothing** like what we expect so we might as well get used to that pause between the comings and goings of life and more and more just live what shows up, moment to moment.

When we open our selves to being more present in the ongoing flow of our life a sense of aliveness enters in that allows us to examine more closely and clearly the transition itself. To move with more flexibility creates choices, and these open to the unexpected in ways that expand how far or where we might go then had we stayed with the plan or an anticipated outcome. This being taken by surprise can create a destination that may stimulate our growth in more ways than could be imagined as we stay open to whatever shows up and allow it to take us to a new place or to a new way of being.

~ Journal for Between the Comings and Goings ~

old – having lived or existed for a long time; familiar or known from the past; accustomed

new – never existing before; appearing, thought of, developed, made, produced for the first time; unfamiliar

Between the Old and New

The old and new, the known and the unknown, the past and the now, and whatever might be emerging. We dance between these realities and sometimes wonder where one starts and the other ends.

There is an overlapping of all the moments of our lives that challenges us to stay in the moment, to be purely present to what is. Nothing more or less than that. Staying alive, being between the old and new, being no longer there but not yet here either, is a task of holding the sense of being pulled away from and going towards at the same time, which actually creates a feeling of standing still.

To live between the old and new is a kind of limbo where you know there is an end and a beginning, but, with one foot in each place, no steps are taken. There is a feeling that you are going through the motions of your life but getting no where for a time. The old informs and the new entices, but there is something watchful in how you stay more and more detached from both.

It is staying with the feelings of being finished with the old long enough while at the same time feeling anticipation for the new in such a way that brings you to the actual between. That place where you discover this standing can bring you a much needed balance.

It is here you are being called to let a certain settling take place in yourself and in your life, before entering the next portal, the next phase, the next span of time, for whatever new is emerging. This place between the old and new has a purpose after all and staying there long enough to feel settled brings you the very balance you need to move forward with more sure footedness, more clarity and certainty, than if you had passed up the opportunity of staying in the in-between for a time. It can be an actual place before decisions are made, steps are taken, new paths entered. It is that psychological open field where you stand balanced and, yes, empty.

When we moved to an island, on undeveloped land, all was blank. The old life had ended but the new had not yet taken form. There was a time of settling in before there was a shape to our lives. This emptying out of the old that gave space for the new to enter in was actually a relief to me.

This place of settling for a time in the space between the old and new can become a kind of energetic emptiness that is full of new yet still unknown potential. This time of settling allows you to eventually dance again in the space between the old and new, sure footed, balanced, in readiness for the next step as finally the next new stone is placed down on your path.

~ Journal for Between the Old and New ~

full – containing as much as possible; having a great deal; well supplied, stocked, or provided; rich or abounding; complete

empty – containing nothing; vacant; without meaning or force; insincere; vain; hungry; to pour out or remove something; having no worth or purpose; useless or unsatisfying; lacking; devoid

Neither Full Nor Empty

You've heard or been asked the question "is your cup half full or half empty?" What does that actually mean? We spend most of our lives living between full and empty; seemingly no different than for the cars we drive. This idea assumes we have an energy tank inside or some kind of an emotional account where you have a sense of feeling full or empty or maybe somewhere in-between. If you fall in that mid-range, then the assumption is that the optimist feels half full and the pessimist half empty.

How might we value these times differently of when you are neither full nor empty? These times when you are maintaining a steady balance of giving and receiving basically what you need, maybe not all you want, but still, most of what you need. In other words, you are satisfied and even content with your lot in life and are just grateful life is moving along and keeping it this way is just fine for now.

A time of no crisis. The seemingly negative or challenging givens of life (as described by David Richo in his 2005 book, <u>The Five Things We Cannot Change…& the Happiness We Find by Embracing Them</u>) are currently at bay and a certain status quo has set in. You find your days pass by with rhythms that have their own kind of pleasure. It's a quality of time we might take for granted, but once one of those challenging givens of life shows up, and the cup empties out, then whether optimist or pessimist, for a time you're just empty. There is little or no gas in the tank and suddenly that status quo of half looks better than anything going on in the moment.

It is in this half measure where we live in harmony between what we want and need that can have its own kind of value. This is where a quantity of time in relative peace can actually have its own quality. It is where "nothing ventured, nothing lost" has benefit and purpose until we find our sea legs and are sent out or go out to sea once again. It is truly a type of pause that can refresh our lives as we regroup and come to terms with what has been, so what is and might yet be can have more clarity.

We are human and we live in time. There has been a past, there is a present moment if you're reading this book, and the future is on the next page. Don't get me wrong, I also believe the power resides more fully in the moment, but it's still a reality that the past can have power over the now and hoping for a better future may be all we have in our empty moments. There is a time to expand and a time to contract. Both are important and valuable.

The times of neither full nor empty serve a higher purpose than we have given them credit for. As you let life settle into a time of status quo it doesn't necessarily mean you are settling or settling for something less than your full potential. It just means you use the half way mark, the mid-point to stay settled long enough to value where you've been in order to see more clearly where you're going. To use this time to be in compassion for yourself and others rather than being driven by the passions that come to the surface of full or to the bottom of empty.

~ Journal for Neither Full Nor Empty ~

enough – as much or as many as necessary, desirable, or tolerable; sufficient

Just Enough

My Mother used to share the saying "How much is enough? Just a little bit more." Isn't that the way of it? So often when we come to that place of enough it triggers, almost compulsively sometimes, that desire for a little bit more. It's like hanging out in enough or just enough isn't enough. It has become a word with negative meaning as if you are somehow settling for less than rather than settling into something quite wonderful.

To be satisfied versus hungry for more, both certainly have their place, but to deeply connect to being satisfied, to feeling that "my needs have been met and I trust they will be met in the future" can open you to feelings of deep security.

In this ever-changing world and our ever-changing lives, feeling secure in having enough can offer a stability that is not only reassuring to yourself and others but can actually provide a foundation for future risk.

When you know what is enough by honoring it and staying with it, there is the opportunity of developing a sense of knowing when to stop or even perhaps when to leave. To know when you have done or said enough, and at minimum when it is time to be still is powerful. You see that getting out of the way allows someone else to go forward into their own world and perhaps in time they will momentarily come back or forward into yours. But it will be connected to that knowing of when enough is enough and acting on that knowledge.

I have come to a time and place in my life where I have gained a new respect for enough. It's not like anger that says STOP. It's more like yield. I yield to my desires and let them pass; let them go on ahead of me. I sit content by the side of the road knowing there will be a time and space for me to move back into the stream of things, but for now it is enough to stop or even to be stopped, neither going forward nor back.

Accepting this place I find myself in that isn't reaching out or protesting, nor is it indifferent. Enough is a place that can instill a deep confidence in the give and take of life, and that on balance I have enough. I am enough, whether you think so or not doesn't really matter. Because I know deep inside I am enough, and just a little bit more might just turn out to be a little too much.

~ Journal for Just Enough ~

silence – refraining from speech or making noise; a collapse of time and space; creating permeable boundaries; oppression; oblivion or obscurity; death; stillness; a state of 'soaring into a new lighter atmosphere weightless and free'; bliss

Silence

What can you say about silence? It seems like a contradiction to write about something that is the absence of sound. In fact silence for me creates a quality of atmosphere that is more like another presence has entered into my space. When you are visited by silence, or you seek it out, there is something magical that happens to your other senses. How strange that when there is silence you can hear a pin drop. Nature noises become music to your ears and bird song a friendly conversation. Water of any sort is like a drug for me. Whether it's rain, a river, waterfall, or ocean waves, water rhythm and its movement going from one place to another soothes me.

Silence opens me up. I get more porous and let down my guard when there is no pressure to say anything. Thoughts come and go as I sit in silence by the stream of consciousness I love so much and time seems to drift and yes, to drag as well.

Silence can trigger the realization I have come to the end of something and that it's time to wait in silence for new instruction. When my mind empties, which is different from when it goes blank into a senior moment, it's the quality of silence that becomes essential to creating quality listening. A span of time and trust to being in a space where I won't be disturbed brings opportunity for silence.

I used to live in a place where there was regular siren sound and five foot set back neighbors so only a long drive to elsewhere gave even a remote chance for silence. Now I live on an island with natural acres around, well off the main road, and silence has become as important and available to me as the air I breathe. It is everywhere I am and a constant companion, broken only by choice. I can now easily take my fill of silence rather than have to seek it out.

This is bliss for me, but I know for others such a reversal from the norm is oppressive. Too much silence, too much of anything really, can create a detachment that threatens rather than soothes. A sensory deprivation is felt and a yearning for contact and stimulation sets in, creating urgency and a restlessness to be away from the silence. A need arises to put an end to the state silence has created in you, so this absence from, is shifted into wanting to be present with the other. You have come to the end of your silence. Your tolerance for solitude has been reached and it begins to feel more like isolation. This is when you leave your silent retreat and re-enter the flow of the main stream as if following your own inner tide table.

Honoring this need for an ebb and flow of silence in your life is part of ancient wisdom. Almost all spiritual practice requires a connection to silence in order to listen for the voice of _____, you fill in the blank. If you believe in the beginning was the Word than before the Word there might have been silence. It is this state where creation begins that reflects our co-creator status which convinces me a certain amount of silence in our lives is essential to health, well being and finding your own unique connection to inspiration. Not that you won't or can't be inspired by other states of being, but I do find silence often is a partner to the inspired moment. The new thought that comes from out of the blue often comes because you have finally reached the silence where the new thought, the word, your word can take form so you are in that moment able to be a co-creator.

~ Journal for Silence ~

spaciousness – having or giving more than enough space or room; vast; extensive; great; large; not confined or limited

Spaciousness

I am looking out at the mountain horizon on a clear day. It is as clear as it can be on an island as it seems clouds are always in the sky. It is here I feel the spaciousness of the landscape I live in. All around me is sky with mountains to the south and ocean to the north. When you live on an island in the middle of the Pacific, spaciousness is built in. So much space wherever you look, I have difficulty understanding when people ask me how I can stand living on such a small island. For me small is a matter of perspective, and also, perhaps I'm not one prone to Rock Fever.

I stand anywhere here and connect instantly to how much space there is, how vast it feels. 2,500 to 4,000 miles of ocean between continents, sky going into infinity as far as I can see, land eighty percent undeveloped so the earth here is full of our natural world, and oceans so deep that the minute you step into the water you enter a whole different wilderness, most of it unexplored. If that isn't spacious, I don't know what is.

The same is true for psychological and spiritual spaciousness. It's a matter of perspective. There are times in my life, and people I have engaged with in the past and now who give me all the space I need. I feel free and able to roam inside myself to my heart's content, and yet there is still love and connection even if they are thousands of miles away. There is a healthy space between us that allows for a lively movement in and out of each others' lives. A knowing that when there is a return much can be shared and exchanged which will usually expand our lives further into feeling even more spacious.

There are times of spiritual enlightenment where I feel the oneness with all life, time and space are suspended, and infinite possibilities flood my consciousness with such excitement and joy I can only sense I have entered a state of bliss. Such moments of grace feel so spacious I can hardly contain myself. I am not meant to be contained or to hold onto anything, but rather to be totally content and deeply grateful to feel so loved.

It is physical, psychological, and spiritual spaciousness that allows us to explore who we are and to enter into the wilderness of our own soul state. When we blessed the land here before building our home, the west held the place of wildness, a part of our land we hadn't cleared. It is this similar place of spacious wild wilderness inside us that holds the possibilities for new perspective, new life, new development. Without this spacious place nothing new or surprising can enter in. This unknown, unexplored inner spacious territory is exactly what is essential for our new growth, for the very thing that keeps us alive. Spaciousness creates the lively energy which expands our conscious potential and our potential for expanded consciousness.

~ Journal for Spaciousness ~

safe – free from damage, danger or injury; giving protection from harm; secure; whole; involving no risk

place – a particular area or locality; region

Safe Place

There are special times when we feel truly safe. Often it is connected to a place inside ourselves, but just as often it can be identified as an actual place we get to and then this feeling of comfort and ease sets in, and suddenly we might notice we're breathing differently and that all is well. For some, this is more easily felt when alone and at other times it can be in the company of someone safe. Someone who gives us this connection to that place in ourselves we can turn to and know we are accepted just as we are. There is no need to explore being anywhere else for a time.

When we arrive at a safe place in our lives, it feels like a gift. Arriving at a state of being that comes to us as grace, a blessing after the storm when we experience our wholeness rather than our injury. We have risen to a moment where we realize we hold the keys to our life and that we can lock or open any door or doors we choose. A moment where we can welcome or close out the other or the experience presented and in that moment of awareness we know that yes, I am safe. I am truly safe to be with myself and I trust this place of arrival. It's not yet time to depart as a safe place is something to be savored. It allows you to take your breath and regroup for the next going out to sea that will call you in its own time and way.

Gratitude settles into your being, thankfulness for this retreat into safety where your wholeness holds the keys and your brokenness can finally be put into safekeeping. It is here that healing begins. There is a need we have to be in our own safe hands while we mend our ways or old/new ways of being mend us. This taking refuge in a safe harbor of our very soul should not be underestimated. We all have need of time to repair in our lives so take full advantage of these times of being anchored in a place of safe harbor.

I remember going to my cousin's weekend home once, in need of a restorative retreat while they were away, and being surrounded by sweet childhood memories. I took a long nap, walked through the small town that led to the sea, made a fire and sat by it with a hot cup of tea upon my return, and in looking up at her shelves of books saw something special. When I opened <u>A Room of One's Own</u> by Virginia Woolf, a life long diary/journal writer, her original signature was written in purple ink on an inside page of this numbered limited first edition. One of the first 100 copies she self published out of her home through Hogarth Press with her husband Leonard. I was so struck by this precious item being safely placed on my cousin's book shelf, hardly noticed between the ordinary, I had no need to explore any further.

    I was safe; this book was in safe keeping hands, and the value of all that was without price. I savored the moment, filled with gratitude to have arrived at this safe harbor, holding and reading at sunset a book written and also once held long enough by Virginia Woolf (1882-1941) so she could sign her name in purple ink on the inside cover back in 1929.

~ Journal for Safe Place ~

anything – no matter of what kind; no matter how much or how little; without limit

possible – capable of existing; that can be in the future; that can be done, known, acquired, selected, used, etc. depending on circumstances; that may be a fact or truth; feasible; likely to be carried through to a successful conclusion, therefore is desirable; potential

Anything Is Possible

Isn't it wonderful when you feel the clouds lift in your life and a new ray of light shines through to instill hope that yes, anything is possible. A new energy comes in to propel you forward, if it only means taking a first step. It may be a step of return or perhaps a response to a call to go in a whole new direction or maybe something in-between. All you know for sure is that something has lifted and in that moment you feel a certain joy returning in even being able to play with the thought that anything is possible.

This can sometimes be tied to our past memories of other similar experiences where we took first steps and life changed. If we've had enough of these experiences, and they led us to positive outcomes, a confidence is built that gives us the courage to risk another step rather than pull back or stop. If on the other hand first steps have caused us to trip and fall, a hesitancy and indecision can enter in and we delay our progress or miss opportunities for new growth that comes when you tie your belief to the thought that anything is possible.

I am not talking about a Pollyanna, rose colored glasses kind of "anything is possible", but rather a deep knowing and trust in your own inner and outer resources that have risen up to call you out of the dark into the light and power of the very idea that anything is possible. It is an expansive moment of consciousness, a waking up after an often necessary time of being asleep.

It is not necessarily a time of awareness, of knowing what is possible, but more an unfocused anything is possible, a time to explore many possibilities without commitment or limiting yourself to something particular. It's what you see children do when they play and imagine all sorts of possibilities, in the face of the ordinary, that makes something extraordinary happen.

This is so much a "being in the moment tied to the future" kind of thing it's hard to pin down. It doesn't want to be pinned down by decision yet, it wants to be played with. Anything is possible is an opening into new worlds of thought and feeling and experience that brings us to the heart of hope. We awaken into a new day without the burden of holding on or holding back. Something has shifted inside or out or both and it's not the same anymore. A difference is felt that is the very thing that has been missing to help us be ready for new awareness.

So stay awhile and absorb and enjoy those moments that personally come to you in life when you intuitively know, without logic, sometimes in the face of great odds, that anything is possible. Realize, believe, and experience how personal this is as you allow your life to be touched by this rare moment of grace.

~ Journal for Anything Is Possible ~

pregnant – full of meaning and significance; filled; abounding; mentally fertile; prolific of ideas; inventive; productive of results

moments – a definite point in time; a brief time of being important or outstanding

Pregnant Moments

Though I've never given birth to a child I've experienced the convergence, the fertilization of the moment when there is this feeling of new life forming inside. It is quite miraculous when we find ourselves in the right time and place, with just the right people, or perhaps alone. This is a time where outer circumstances converge to fertilize the moment with extraordinary potential and you feel a certain magic infuse the life you're living so you know new choices are available and change is not far behind.

These moments are full of something mysterious that can't quite be explained or fully understood. All you know for sure is that you've received this infusion of new life which expands your experience to feel there is now more than you had anticipated come to assist you on your journey.

I am reminded of a night with friends where we shared a full moon bonfire and a bit of rain started to fall. A moment came when I thought the elements would converge to extinguish the light and the warmth of our fire. Instead the elements converged and the full moon rose up over the hillside. Across the bay, through the mist, a night rainbow appeared giving us this rare and ancient pregnant moment. It felt like a visitation from the ancestors, from powers traveling across time and space to infuse a certain magic into our lives, and to assist us in believing that what might be thought of as a myth of the past is actually power available for us today.

We can have extraordinary experiences if we stay awake and aware and don't have our backs turned away, because on that night our backs were turned away from the night rainbow. It was another in our group looking for more wood to fuel our small fire that saw and shared with us this pregnant moment. That generosity of spirit and a special excitement seem to go hand and hand with pregnant moments. You can hardly keep from brimming over as the fullness enters into your life and something is given rather than taken away. A deep sense of fertility energizes and enters you, inspiring new thoughts, new ways of being, new life forming, just as a new day dawns or a full moon rises over the hillside as your fire burns on in the rain.

~ **Journal for Pregnant Moments** ~

peace – harmony; an undisturbed state of mind; serenity; calm; quiet; tranquility; to become silent; end hostilities; a treaty or freedom from war

Peace

I've come to the shoreline at mid day to write about peace. A simple word for a big subject. It seems bold to think I have anything unique to add to the body of work that has been written about peace. I'm leaning up against a sand bank with the tide changing from high to low as a lone surfer sits in the water. My dog, Sufi, is chasing sand crabs and the waves breaking even and clear make me feel like there is indeed peace here at Kalihiwai Bay.

How to describe this feeling of being cradled, held, at peace. No need to go anywhere or do anything, just being in the moment where peace is and letting it come to rest inside me. Taking it all in as I settle down in the sand and let the earth support me as that board supports the surfer on a wave as an easy stance glides him to shore.

Peace can be that moment where you catch a perfect wave which effortlessly takes you beyond where you've ever been. It has movement and a certain power, this peace. A non-violent intervention that takes you to a new or sometimes vaguely familiar place in your life that comes from accepting who you are. Whatever is happening is somehow meaningfully connected to your life's purpose. There is an alignment with what is that is unique and true in ways that bring you peace, it can feel like a gift.

This peace can't be sought after or forced or demanded. It just shows up at moments in our life when all is well and an assurance comes into our mind and heart, bringing with it a confidence born of peace. It's akin to grace; living within the design of your life where you know what you know and for now it is all you need.

There is still mystery, the unknown and change will come soon enough, but underneath all that, at a deeper level there is peace. You may still feel the turbulence of the wave overhead but if you dive deep enough there is peace at the bottom of it all. There is also certainly more peace while coming to the end of something you realize it's time to express and stand up for your own bottom line. The power and peace of that decisive action can then glide you to shore as you stand up for yourself and say from the depths of your soul, peace be with you.

~ Journal for Peace ~

stillness – hushed, soft, or low in sound; not moving; stationary; at rest; motionless; serene; not effervescent or bubbling

in-between – in or through the space or time that separates two things; along a course that connects or relates to; in the interval

Stillness of the In-between

I have discovered arriving at the stillness of the in-between is a real destination. It can be a place inside that I return to again and again as I journey home. There is an urge to lay anchor in this safe harbor of my soul and wait out the calm or the storm. It is a place between too little or too much where I come to rest and let the stillness enter in to hold me, and steady me in readiness for recognizing what is just right or just enough.

It is here in this safe harbor where I let the stillness restore, replenish, or repair whatever has been extreme or neglected in my life. Life stress has caught up with me and only the stillness of the in-between contains the antidote for a cure. I am compelled in these moments to stop all movement and divest myself of any willfulness or intention and just absorb the stillness, the very essence of nothing, no thing. I feel its value weigh in on me and take over my life. It demands everything, total surrender and a deep trust before I can even have the possibility of entering this stillness.

It is here you too may realize, as you've laid down anchor in your soul, you've actually laid down what has been weighing you down. By this very act you are brought to the stillness of the in-between. The very stillness needed to eventually lift the weight, the heaviness, the burden of the pain, the grief, the fear that steered you to safe harbor in the first place.

You realize your feelings can navigate you to the stillness of a safe harbor and that they are your protection. To stay connected to your anchor is essential. To feel the weight of your feelings and respond to them with care is your survival. The very weight of your feelings can anchor you; steady you in preparation for the going out to sea once again.

When you come to the end of this stillness, when you are ready to lift anchor, you now have a new strength and vision to do so at a time between the tides when going out to sea is full of possibilities. You venture out into the currents of your new life restored, centered into your own true north, no longer lost, but headed once again toward home, to the place where you are welcomed and seen for who you are. In this stillness you have been seen, recognized, loved from within, and it has made all the difference.

~ Journal for Stillness of the In-between ~

~ My heartfelt gratitude to ~

Tiffany Noel Buchanan for blessing this project with her tears.

Maggie Burdge for our beloved lifelong friendship felt whether near or far.

Saim Caglayan for living and sharing the creative spirit with me all these years.

Mckayleh Bonni Halingten for her ongoing wise counsel and enthusiasm.

Marisa Kennedy Miller for editing and guiding this project to completion.

William Daniel Francis Perri for his confidence and ongoing encouragement.

Patricia Margaret Rouen my friend and fellow traveler through both joy and sorrow.

Michael Stillwater for inspiring the stillness of the in-between.

Frances Pauline Woods for her warm spirit and kind photograph.

My Circle of Friends for always supporting and accepting me through their love.

```
    N
W + E
    S
```

New Moon
Kalihiwai Ridge
Kaua`i, Hawai`i
Enjoy God

Maggie Lea

Maggie Lea, psychologist, resides on the island of Kaua`i. She facilitates a yearly women's retreat, the North Shore Caregivers Support Group, and seeing individuals in her lakeside gazebo on Kalihiwai Ridge. She loves reading, writing, doing family genealogy for her friends, playing Mah Jongg, a bit of travel now and then, but best of all swimming in Kalihiwai Bay as her dog, Sufi, watches from shore.

To contact the author email
maggielea@timebetweenthetides.com

To order books on web site go to
www.timebetweenthetides.com

Kalihiwai Moonrise
Cover oil painting by Saim Caglayan
www.saimcaglayan.com   www.hanapepeartworks.com

Photo by Frances Woods
www.kauai-photographer.com

Definitions
Webster's New World Dictionary
3rd College Edition

www.ingramcontent.com/pod-product-compliance
Lightning Source LLC
Chambersburg PA
CBHW020008050426
42450CB00005B/363